ICE STORM!

The 1998 Freeze

by Bob Temple

Consultant: Daniel H. Franck, Ph.D.

BEARPORT
PUBLISHING

New York, New York

Credits

Front Cover (background), © Dick Blume, Syracuse Newspapers / AP Images, (inset) Bill Sikes / AP Images; Back Cover (background), © Tom Hanson / AP Images.

Title page, © Bill Sikes / AP Images; 4–5, © Gordon Beck, The Gazette, Montreal; 7, © Michel St. Jean, La Voix de l'Est; 8, © Nashville Room Historic Photo Collection, Nashville Public Library; 9, © Andre Pichette; 11, © Robert Skinner, La Presse; 12, © Tom Hanson / AP Images; 13, © AP Photo / Michael Okoniewski; 14, © Andre Pichette; 15, © Deanna Clark, Brockville (Ontario) Recorder and Times; 16, © Phil Norton; 17, © Robert F. Bukaty / AP Images; 18, © Ryan Remiorz / AP Images; 19, © Robert Laaberge, / AFP / Getty Images; 20, © Armand Trottier, La Presse; 21, © Drew Gragg, Ottawa Citizen; 22, © Alain Dion, La Voix de l'Est; 23, © John Mahoney, The Gazette, Montreal; 24, © Marcos Townsend, The Gazette, Montreal; 25, © Martin Chaberland, La Presse; 26, © Christopher Morris / Corbis; 27, © Richard T. Nowitz, National Geographic / Getty Images; 29, © John Jensenius / NOAA.

Publisher: Kenn Goin
Project Editor: Lisa Wiseman
Creative Director: Spencer Brinker
Photo Researcher: Amy Dunleavy
Original Design: Dawn Beard Creative and Triesta Hall of Blu–Design

Library of Congress Cataloging-in-Publication Data

Ice storm! : the 1998 freeze / by Bob Temple ; consultant, Daniel H. Franck.
    p. cm.
 Includes bibliographical references and index.
 ISBN-13: 978-1-59716-275-3 (lib. bdg.)
 ISBN-10: 1-59716-275-2 (lib. bdg.)
 ISBN-13: 978-1-59716-303-3 (pbk.)
 ISBN-10: 1-59716-303-1 (pbk.)
 1. Ice storms—Canada, Eastern—Juvenile literature. 2. Ice storms—New England—Juvenile literature. 3. Ice storms—New York (State) —Juvenile literature.

 QC926.45.C2 I25 2007
 363.34'926097—dc22

2006007210

For more information, write to Bearport Publishing Company, Inc., 101 Fifth Avenue, Suite 6R, New York, New York 10003. Printed in the United States of America.

10 9 8 7 6 5 4 3 2 1

Table of Contents

The Beginning

A noise that sounded like gunfire filled the air. Startled, Alex woke up. He looked around and saw that his alarm clock wasn't working. He thought that the power must be out. Suddenly, a strange orange-blue light flashed outside. What was going on?

Major ice storms happen about once every 50 years.

Alex jumped out of bed and ran to the window. Outside, a cold, freezing rain fell. Thick layers of ice covered the trees in his yard. The weight of the ice was too much for the branches. They began to bend and snap and crash to the ground. Then the power lines started to short out, creating a colorful light show. Soon, they were falling down, too. An ice storm had begun!

▲ Alex and his family lived across the river from Montreal, Canada, in a city called Saint-Lambert (shown here). The ice storm began on Monday, January 5, 1998. The temperature was about 18°F (-8°C).

What Is an Ice Storm?

For bad weather to be called an ice storm, freezing rain must fall for several hours. The rain must coat surfaces, such as roads and tree branches, with ice that is at least ¼ inch (.6 cm) thick.

How the Ice Storm Formed

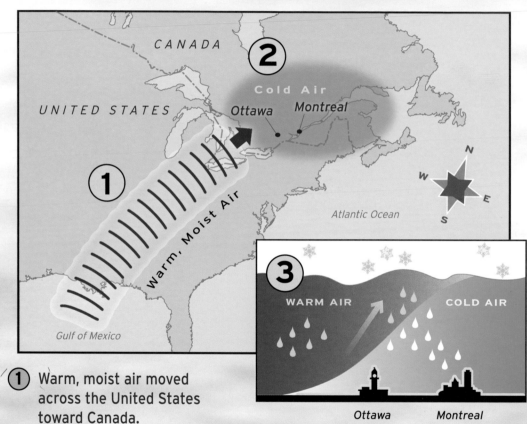

① Warm, moist air moved across the United States toward Canada.

② The moist air mass bumped into a cold air mass that was standing still, causing snow to form.

③ As the snow fell, it moved through the warm air beneath it and changed to rain high over Montreal and Ottawa. Then as the rain passed through the layer of cold air close to the ground, it became freezing rain. It turned into ice as soon as it hit objects, such as trees and roads, that were 32°F (0°C) or colder.

The Great Ice Storm of 1998 was brutal. The storm lasted for five days. The freezing rain fell for more than 80 hours. Some areas were coated with ice that was three to four inches (8 to 10 cm) thick.

◀ The storm's ice covered everything it touched, including this mailbox in Quebec, Canada.

During the 1998 storm, rain didn't fall continuously. Sometimes the rain turned into snow or stopped altogether.

January Thaw

In Canada and **New England**, freezing rain is common during December and January. It often occurs early in the morning, the coldest time of the day. The rain usually lasts for only a short period of time.

▲ Ice storms can happen even in the Southern United States. The Great Ice Storm of 1951 hit states from Louisiana up to Ohio. This street in Tennessee got lots of snow and ice.

The freezing rain that began on January 5, 1998, was different. The day before, an unusually warm weather system formed over the eastern part of North America. In fact, weather forecasters expected that temperatures would rise above freezing. They even **predicted** a January **thaw**. However, it turned out that the conditions were right for something quite different—a major ice storm.

▲ The 1998 ice storm hits Montreal, Canada.

Predicting ice storms can be tricky. It's hard to tell when the warm and cold air will mix in just the right way to cause freezing rain.

The Storm Hits

The 1998 ice storm covered parts of Canada, New England, and New York. However, Canada was hit the hardest by the storm. There, about 28 people died and over 900 were hurt. Millions of trees and up to 30,000 electrical poles fell down under the weight of the ice. More than four million people lost power.

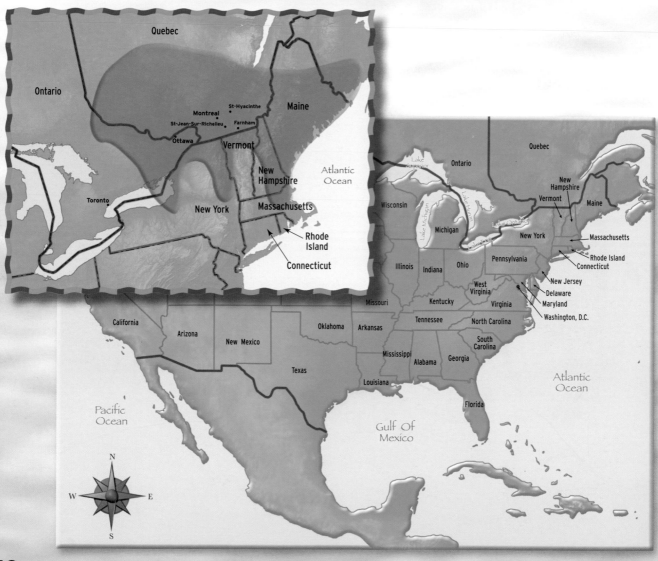

The storm did not hit the United States as hard. Only half a million homes lost electricity. There were also far fewer deaths. Damage in the United States totaled about $450 million. In Canada, the cost was greater. The storm was the most expensive natural disaster in the country's history. It caused billions of dollars in damage.

▲ An icy street in Montreal, Canada

Two weeks after the Great Ice Storm of 1998 hit, another ice storm struck New England. Thousands of homes lost power.

The Storm Continues

After the first day, Alex hoped the storm would pass quickly. The next day, however, the storm showed no signs of slowing down. Power lines and trees continued to crash to the ground, snapping from the weight of the ice.

◀ Stefan Kubiseski and his dog, Jedi, tried to avoid the fallen power lines as they walked down the street in Ottawa, Canada.

The **frigid** temperatures and thick ice made travel difficult and dangerous. Ice covered the roads, making them very slippery. Tree branches and other **debris** littered the streets. The cleaning crews were unable to clear the roads quickly.

▲ Icy streets and fallen branches left many people stranded at home.

Each tree branch held ice that was 20 to 30 times heavier than its own weight.

Wanted: Generators

The storm forced schools and businesses to close. People stayed home and waited for conditions to get better. The ice-coated land looked pretty. However, without electricity, heat, or running water, everyday life became very hard.

▼ Though extremely dangerous, the icy conditions made everything look like a winter wonderland.

Some people used fireplaces or wood-burning stoves to keep their houses warm. Others used gas-powered **generators**. However, people still had a tough time. It was not easy to get gas because most fuel stations had closed. Deliveries couldn't be made due to the poor road conditions. People who wanted to buy generators were out of luck. Stores ran out of them within the first few days of the storm.

▲ In some areas, drivers waited for hours to buy gas.

A year after the storm, woodstoves and generators still sold so quickly that many stores couldn't keep them in stock.

Cold and Frustrated

Children thought the storm was fun. They got to stay home from school. They could even ice-skate in the streets! Many families tried to make the best of the storm. They used backyard grills or camp stoves to cook meals. They played cards and told stories by candlelight.

▲ These kids set up a hockey rink in a frozen cornfield.

People had to use umbrellas when they went outside to protect themselves from falling tree branches as well as the icy rain.

Soon, however, people started to grow tired of "camping out" in their own homes. Many houses had been damaged by the falling trees and branches. Water began to leak through tears in people's roofs. However, there was not much anyone could do about the storm but wait for it to end.

▲ Hannah Wilbur of Freeport, Maine, had to do her history homework by candlelight during the storm.

Freezing to Death

Soon, many homes became so cold that families had no choice but to leave them. Alex and his family moved into a hotel. Many cities opened shelters in school gyms and church basements that still had power. There, people could sleep, eat, and shower.

▲ Hundreds of thousands of residents moved into shelters during the storm.

Other families, however, wanted to stay and take care of their homes. As these houses grew colder and colder, some people developed **hypothermia**. After a while, their bodies became so cold that they died.

◄ People getting free food at a shelter in Montreal, Canada

In Canada, some shelters became so crowded that there were **influenza** outbreaks. Flu shots were soon given to people to keep them healthy.

19

Triangle of Darkness

Most people in Canada were without electricity for days. However, one part of Montreal went without power for much longer. People were still in the dark one month after the storm ended. This area became known as the Triangle of Darkness.

▲ The Triangle of Darkness included the cities of Saint-Hyacinthe, Farnham, and Saint-Jean-sur-Richelieu (shown here).

Farmers outside of Montreal suffered greatly, too. They relied on electricity to operate milk machines. They also needed power to heat their buildings. Farmers worried that their livestock might freeze to death. Many farmers lost their water supplies, causing animals to suffer and die.

Without power, dairy farmers couldn't keep milk at the right temperature. They were forced to pour out millions of gallons (liters) of soured milk.

◀ Farm machines that were left outside during the storm could not be used because they were covered in ice.

A State of Emergency

On January 8, the government of Canada declared a **state of emergency**. The Army arrived to help. For many days, soldiers helped deliver supplies to the areas most in need. They worked with crews to fix power lines and remove snow and ice.

▲ Even crews from Connecticut came to help the people of Quebec, Canada.

People from many different places helped out during the crisis. **Donations** of blankets, food, and money poured in. Communities helped run shelters. People delivered and set up generators. They brought hot meals to the work crews. Everyone worked together toward one goal—to get through the storm. Slowly, life started to return to normal.

▲ Isabelle Guibert of Quebec, Canada, tries to scrape the ice off her car.

In the United States, **federal** disaster areas were declared in Maine, New Hampshire, Vermont, and New York. The **National Guard** was sent to help these states.

The Storm Ends

On January 10, the freezing rain finally stopped. For some, however, it was too late. Many businesses, farms, and parks didn't survive the storm. The trees and forests would need years to recover from all the damage. Cleaning up the debris would take months.

▲ This machine helped to break up the thick layers of ice on the Richelieu River in Quebec, Canada.

Quebec makes about 70 percent of the world's maple syrup. Many of the trees, which produce the syrup, were destroyed by the storm.

In Canada, damage to the electrical lines was so bad that they couldn't even be repaired. The whole system needed to be rebuilt.

▼ The large towers that held electrical lines tumbled under the weight of the ice.

Changes

The Great Ice Storm of 1998 brought about many changes. Governments in both Canada and the United States have developed new emergency plans to keep people safe. Power companies have made their electrical lines stronger. In some areas, lines are now buried underground.

◀ Montreal, Canada, during the storm

Alex's family was lucky. Power was restored to their house after eight days. They had lots of tree limbs to clear away and a few repairs to make on their roof. Soon, however, life was back to normal. Like most people who lived through the Great Ice Storm of 1998, they would be better prepared for the next big freeze.

▲ Montreal, Canada, years after the storm

During the storm, water plants lost power. Officials then worried that the drinking water might be **contaminated.** They told people to boil water before they used it to make sure it was safe to drink.

27

Just the Facts

- **The Great Arctic Outbreak of 1899**—An extreme cold wave in the eastern half of the United States caused one of the worst blizzard-and-ice storms ever recorded in the United States. In New Orleans, Louisiana, the temperature fell to 7°F (-14°C). Snow was reported as far south as Fort Myers, Florida. Huge amounts of ice flowed through the Mississippi River, causing flooding.

- **The Great Ice Storm of 1951**—From Louisiana to Ohio, this storm raged for several days. The livestock, crops, and fruit trees it damaged led to losses of more than $100 million. During the storm, about 25 people died and 500 were injured.

Damage Caused by the Great Ice Storm of 1998:
- More than 40 people died.
- More than 4 million people lost electricity.
- The estimated cost of the storm was more than $5.4 billion.
- About 600,000 people were forced to leave their homes.
- Millions of acres of trees were damaged or destroyed.
- More than 30,000 electrical poles fell.

Improvements Because of the Great Ice Storm of 1998:

- Enhanced weather forecasting equipment
- Improved power systems to prevent failures
- Better emergency plans
- More generators bought for homes

Emergency Winter Supplies Needed to Survive an Ice Storm:

- a flashlight with extra batteries
- a portable radio
- lots of canned food and several bottles of water
- first-aid supplies and extra medicine
- heating fuel (such as wood)
- woodstove or generator
- fire extinguisher
- smoke and carbon monoxide detectors

▲ An icy road in Portland, Maine, during the storm

Glossary

contaminated (kuhn-TAM-uh-*nay*-tid) when something is dirty or should not be used

debris (duh-BREE) scattered pieces of houses, buildings, and other objects left after a storm

donations (doh-NAY-shuns) gifts of money or supplies to help people in need

federal (FED-ur-uhl) having to do with the government of a nation; not a local government

frigid (FRIJ-id) very cold

generators (JEN-uh-*ray*-turz) machines that produce electricity

hypothermia (*hye*-puh-THUR-mee-uh) a condition in which a person's body temperature has become dangerously low

influenza (*in*-floo-EN-zuh) the flu; an illness caused by a virus; symptoms include fever and muscle pain

National Guard (NASH-uh-nuhl GARD) voluntary military groups found in every state in the United States; each group is controlled by the governor of the particular state

New England (NOO ING-gluhnd) a region of the Northeastern United States made up of six states: Maine, New Hampshire, Vermont, Massachusetts, Rhode Island, and Connecticut

predicted (pri-DIK-tid) said what could happen in the future

state of emergency (STATE UHV i-MUR-juhn-see) a condition in which a government calls for extra help from the military or law enforcement to respond to a crisis

thaw (THAW) a melting

Bibliography

Abley, Mark. *The Ice Storm: An Historic Record in Photographs of January 1998.* Toronto: McClelland & Stewart (1998).

Phillips, David, Michael Parfit, and Suzanne Chisholm. *Blame It on the Weather: Amazing Weather Facts.* San Diego, CA: Portable Press (1998).

* archives.cbc.ca/IDD-1-70-258/disasters_tragedies/ice_storm/
* canadaonline.about.com/cs/weather/p/icestorm.htm
* windupradio.com/icestorm.htm
* www.islandnet.com/~see/weather/elements/icestorm.htm

Read More

Scheff, Duncan. *Ice Storms and Hailstorms.* Orlando, FL: Raintree (2001).

Ylvisaker, Anne. *Ice Storms.* Mankato, MN: Capstone Press (2003).

Learn More Online

Visit these Web sites to learn more about ice storms:
* library.thinkquest.org/03oct/01027/icestorm.html
* www.msc-smc.ec.gc.ca/media/icestorm98/icestorm98_the_worst_e.cfm

Index

About the Author

Bob Temple is the author of more than 40 fiction and nonfiction books for children. He lives with his family in the Twin Cities area of Minnesota.